MAGICAL WISHES

The Adventures of

Goopy & Bagha

AF655548

Written by Gulzar

Gulzar, an eminent writer of rare talent, is also a leading filmmaker, lyricist and scriptwriter. The prestigious Sahitya Akademi Award was conferred upon him in 2002 for his collection of short stories, *Dhuan*. Gulzar has authored several collections of poems and short stories in Urdu. Well-known for his books for children, his creative repertoire also includes plays, ballets, translations and music albums. Gulzar was honoured with the Lifetime Achievement Award for his contribution to Hindi cinema in 2002 and with the Padma Bhushan in 2004. He also received an Oscar (2008), and a Grammy (2010) for his song in the film *Slumdog Millionaire*.
His books for Scholastic include, *Kayada*, *Ek Mein Do*, *Potli Baba ki Kahani*: *Mangu aur Mangli* and *Potli Baba ki Kahani*: *Goopy Gyne Bagha Byne*.

Illustrated by Shilpa Ranade

After studying animation at the Royal College of Art, London, Shilpa Ranade directed short animation films for Channel 4, UK. Her films have travelled all over the world, winning accolades at prestigious film festivals. She is a founding member of Damaru, a project involved in creating content for children. During the last decade, Shilpa has illustrated numerous children's books for various publishers. She is currently teaching animation at IDC, IIT Bombay, and is making *Goopi Gavaiyaa Bagha Bajaiyaa*, an animated feature film for the Children's Film Society of India.

For Samay, Bosky and Govind

MAGICAL WISHES

The Adventures of

Goopy & Bagha

Written by Gulzar

Retold by Samina Mishra
Illustrated by Shilpa Ranade
Designed by Soumitra Ranade

SCHOLASTIC
New York Toronto London Auckland
Sydney New Delhi Hong Kong

It was night – black, dark and silent.
Goopy sat huddled in the hollow of a tree in a forest, dense and deep. The animals of the forest were either fast asleep or mute with fear.

Goopy shuddered.

High on his perch on a sheesham tree,
Bagha sighed. There was only one way to beat the dark, silent night, he decided. He straightened his dholak and struck it once.

Dhak.

In his hollow, Goopy strained his ears.
A faint beat of a drum seemed to carry through the air– dhak, dhak-dhak, dhak. There it was again.
Dhak, dhak-dhak, dhak.

Goopy opened his mouth and out popped notes of the alaap – sa re ga ma.
The drumming became louder.
Dhak dhak dhak dhak.
Goopy sat up and sang louder – pa dha ni sa.
Dhak dhak dhak dhak.

Sa ni dha pa...
Dhak dhak dhak dhak,
Ma ga re sa...
Dhak dhak dhak dhak.

The voice and the drum created a musical duet. Bagha climbed down with his dholak and walked towards the singing voice. Goopy emerged from the hollow and walked towards the drumming. Pushing aside vines, ducking under branches, the two came up to either side of an old banyan tree. Singing and beating the dholak in time, the two circled the tree and – dhak! They came face to face with each other. Goopy shut his mouth. Bagha stopped beating the drum. They stared at each other in the dark, silent night.

Then they both spoke, at once.
'Who are you?'
'What are you doing here?'
'Sorry, after you,' said Goopy.
'No, no, after you,' said Bagha.
'Alright, if you insist. I am Goopy, son of a village grocer and singer by temperament. Alas, my family and the villagers have no appreciation for the finer things of life. Whenever I sing— which is very often— they shout at me to shut up.'

'Oh no, that's just like my story!' exclaimed Bagha,
'I am Bagha, also a musician by temperament—and skill,
as you've just heard.'

'Last night, I was singing on my terrace,' Goopy continued,
'an enchanting raag bageshri, and you'll never believe it,
this rabble of villagers came out with sticks to make me shut up.
They forced me to leave the village and so, here I am, alone but
for my music. And now, of course, you.'

Bagha shook his head sadly,
'I was thrown out of my village
for drumming all the time.
But, music is my life—
how can it have a timetable?'

Goopy and Bagha consoled each other.
'What we need to find is a true
appreciator of music,'
began Goopy, 'a patron of the arts ...'
'A king? I have heard that
they keep musicians in their court.'
'What a fine idea, Bagha!'
exclaimed Goopy. 'Come, let's go to
the river.'
'Why?'
'Because, my clever comrade,
the king's palace is on the other side!'

So, Goopy and Bagha made their way down to the river. Dawn was breaking. A cock crowed in the distance and birds chirped. The day promised to be a good one. Goopy broke into raag bhairav. Bagha started drumming happily. As he picked up the tempo, he began to hop along to the beat. His eyes were closed and he had a big smile on his face as he savoured the music.
And then – splash!

Bagha opened his eyes to find that he had fallen into the river.
'Goopy!' he cried out, happily. 'Here's the river. Let's cross it.'
Goopy stood uncertainly at the riverbank, raag bhairav on pause.
'But ... I can't swim,' he said.
'Neither can I,' laughed Bagha.
'But the river can. She will carry us. Jump in!'
Bagha waved enthusiastically from the river.
Goopy watched him floating away, took a deep breath,
shut his eyes, and with a quick prayer, flung himself into the water.

Goopy and Bagha held hands as the river tossed them around. All day, the two ducked, turned cartwheels in the water and almost drowned. The drum around Bagha's neck bobbed along the water, keeping them afloat. At last, they came to the other edge of the river, to another dark and silent forest. Darkness had begun to fall, and the two friends shivered in their wet clothes.

'So, where's this palace?' croaked Bagha, rubbing his hands together to warm himself.

Before Goopy could answer, a voice spoke out in a commanding tone, 'Go straight and turn right.'

Trembling, Goopy and Bagha stared at each other with eyes as large as tablas.

'Goopy!'

'Bagha!'

'Who was that?'

The voice spoke again,

'I am the king's sentry. Do as I say or else you'll be taken forcibly.'

Goopy and Bagha stumbled ahead, holding on to each other. Sometimes, Goopy pulled Bagha along, sometimes Bagha pushed Goopy on.
'Turn right here,' commanded the voice.
Just as they turned, Goopy and Bagha were astonished to see that the trees in the grove all had eyes and the eyes were glaring at them. They turned around and found that the jungle was suddenly teeming with people. Wild-looking people with wet, dripping clothes and hair.

'Who are you?' growled one of them.
'This is Goopy, he sings.'
'This is Bagha, he plays the drum.'
'And who are you?' said the two together.
'We are ghosts—drowned ghosts!'
Goopy and Bagha turned pale.
'Wh ... wha ... what is that?' quavered Bagha.
'All of us died by drowning. This is a forest of drowned ghosts.'
'Oh no! We're dead!' whispered Bagha.
'Don't lie!' yelled the sentry, 'You're not dead. I was watching the whole time. You almost drowned but then this drum saved you. Now, come to the king!'

The sentry called out a spell:
'Splish splash sploosh!
Away with a whoosh,
To the king's court we go
Goopy and Bagha in tow.'

In the blink of an eye, Goopy and Bagha were transported
straight to the Ghost King. He stood there, resplendent
in multiple eyes. He had eyes everywhere—two pairs on his face,
a pair on his shoulders, a pair on his chest and even a pair on his knees.

'Ah! So you survived. Didn't drown, eh?'
'No, sir, king ... Please let us go,' croaked Goopy and Bagha in fear.
'We'll let you go, we'll let you go. But, not tonight.
Tonight you will make music for my daughter's wedding.
And tomorrow, you shall be free to go.'

So, Goopy sang, Bagha drummed and the ghosts danced.
The Ghost King's daughter was married off and Goopy and Bagha
made music to their heart's content, with no one shushing them
or stopping them or asking them to be quiet. Finally, the two friends
fell in a heap, fast asleep.

The next morning when they awoke, there was no sign of the ghosts.
The eyes on the trees had disappeared. The forest was still.
Goopy rubbed his eyes and turned to Bagha,
'What a night of music! You played so well.'
'And you sang so well!' declared Bagha. 'Everyone was entranced.'
'I wish it would always be like that when we made music,' said Goopy, wistfully.
Suddenly, the Ghost King's voice rang out. 'It will be. It will always be like that.
Whenever Goopy and Bagha make music together, the listener will be entranced.'
Pleased with Goopy and Bagha's performance, he bestowed a boon upon the two
and gave them a pair of shoes that could transport them anywhere.
'Use them well,' he declared, 'And whenever you wish for anything, just say –
"Sploosh splash splish, give us what we wish." Then raise one hand each and clap
them together. Your wish will come true.'
Goopy and Bagha's eyes sparkled as they thanked him. The Ghost King vanished
and Goopy and Bagha decided to try the spell.
'Let's go to an orchard,' said Bagha. Raising their hands, the two chanted:
'Sploosh splash splish,
Give us what we wish.
An orchard to rest in and delicacies to eat
Make us content, perform this feat.'

Lo and behold, as they clapped their hands together, they found themselves in a fruit-laden orchard, with a picnic laid out. Goopy and Bagha ate and drank their fill. Then, putting on their magic shoes, they decided to go to the palace of the kingdom they were in.

Clap!

The gates of the palace towered above them. The two sentries at the gate sneered at Goopy and Bagha,
'Where are you two country bumpkins off to?'
'To see the king,' said Goopy,
'I am Goopy Gyne and this is Bagha Byne. We want to meet the king.'
'Do you think anyone can just walk in and meet the king?'
The sentries roared with laughter.
'Why not?' said Goopy, winking at Bagha.

Clap!

The next moment, Goopy and Bagha were in the bedroom of the King of Shundi. King Shundi and Queen Shundi were eating grapes and gossiping about their neighbour, the ruler of Halla.
'What kind of king is he, always listening to music!' said King Shundi, scornfully.
'I know! Take my advice – annex his kingdom,' said the Queen.
'Good idea! But what will I do with all those musicians in his court?'
'Oh, just drown them in the well. And if there are any left over, hang them from the trees.'

Goopy and Bagha listened at the doorway and realised this was the wrong kingdom for them. Just then, Queen Shundi looked up and caught sight of them. 'Intruders!' she shrieked. 'Catch those men!' Goopy and Bagha ran helter-skelter, but alas, they were caught by sentries, marched straight off to prison and locked-up in neighbouring cells. The king sentenced them to death by hanging early the next morning. Bagha's drum was to be burnt at the same spot.

Bagha wailed in his cell, lamenting the loss of his drum.
'Stop it, Bagha! We're about to die and you're crying for your drum!'
Goopy said, exasperatedly,
'But, Goopy, what can we do?'
'Think, Bagha, think. We will be together for the hanging ...'
'Yes, but ...' began Bagha. And then he smiled.
'Ah!'

Early the next morning, Goopy and Bagha were led to the town square where a platform had been erected. Two nooses hung in the centre of a crowd of people. On the side was a pyre of sticks on which the drum had been placed. King Shundi and Queen Shundi sat on high chairs to get a good view of the proceedings. A match was struck and the pyre lit. As the flames started to travel up towards the drum,
King Shundi thundered, 'Do you have any last requests?'

Goopy and Bagha exchanged looks and Goopy spoke up,
'O King, we are childhood friends. Please let us embrace one last time.'
'We will allow it,' said the King with an evil smile.
So, Goopy and Bagha's hands were untied and they approached each other.
Goopy winked and raised his hand. Bagha smiled and raised his.
Then, both shouted out,

'Sploosh splash splish,
Give us what we wish.
Away from here we go
With Bagha's drum in tow!'

Clap!

The next moment, they were back near the tree where they had first met. They laughed and danced in joy. Bagha took up his drum and Goopy started singing. So lost were they in their music that they did not notice a band of dacoits that entered the forest with a princess they had kidnapped, bound in a sack. The music worked its magic and the dacoits stood still, listening. The sack rolled off the horse but the dacoits paid no attention to it. A king and his soldiers came chasing behind the dacoits. They too stood entranced by the music.

When the song ended and the spell was broken, the dacoits looked at the king and his soldiers, gave a cry and galloped away on their horses, leaving the sackful of princess behind. The king rushed to untie the sack and freed his daughter.

Turning to Goopy and Bagha, he thanked them profusely.

'Ah! There is magic in your music. Your music saved my daughter.'

He was King Halla. Rewarding Goopy and Bagha with a bagful of gold coins and two horses, he bade them return with him and join his court.

'Sir, we can arrive there in the clap of ...' began Bagha, proudly.

'Bagha!' cut in Goopy, glaring at him. 'Of course, we will do as the king says.'

Bagha looked a bit confused and then understanding dawned.

'Oh ... yes, of course.'

So, Goopy and Bagha got on the horses and followed King Halla and his troupe. When they arrived at the palace, they were greeted with much fanfare. The princess, it turned out, had a twin sister, and King Halla made the two princesses take special care of Goopy and Bagha. A day of celebration was announced in the Halla court and the two musicians were at the centre of much merriment. They sang, danced and drummed with the courtiers. The princesses stood to one side, listening to the music and exchanging coy glances with Goopy and Bagha. King Halla saw them and smiled knowingly.

Just then, the Prime Minister entered the court and shouted for the music to stop.

'Your Excellency, I have grave news,' he declared. 'We are under attack. King Shundi has surrounded the palace from all sides. Our soldiers are fighting back bravely, but I fear we do not stand a chance. It is time for you and the princesses to leave the palace through the secret tunnel.' King Halla grabbed his daughters by the hand and asked Goopy and Bagha to follow him.

Bagha turned to Goopy and said, 'Goopy, this is not a time for us to run away. It's a test for us and our music.'

Goopy nodded, 'You're right. We must stay and fight.'

The princesses tried to reason with them, 'This is not a time for music. It is war!'

'There is always a time for music,' said Bagha.

'And now is the time for a song of destruction,' declared Goopy.

Saying goodbye to the stunned King Halla and the princesses, Goopy and Bagha ran to the terrace of the palace. There was an army of soldiers swarming around with bows, arrows and other weapons. One side of the palace had caught fire, and King Shundi sat atop an elephant, watching the havoc he had caused. An arrow of rage shot through Bagha and he started to drum, loud and fast. Goopy joined in, his voice in rhythm with the beat of the drum.

As they picked up the tempo, the soldiers froze in mid-action. Slowly, spellbound by the music, they stopped fighting. Goopy and Bagha, in full musical stride, clapped their hands together and jumped from the terrace to the battlefield. Clap! They were on the palace tower. Clap! They were astride a cavalryman's shoulder. Everyone kept turning their heads in shock as the two disappeared and appeared magically. Finally, they landed on the king's elephant. King Shundi and the elephant's mahout were in a musical trance. Goopy and Bagha eased off the rope from the elephant's howdah and bound the king's hands and feet. Grabbing him from either end, they chanted the spell and clapped their hands.

After the music stopped, the magic began to wear off and the armies started to come back to normal. When they looked towards King Shundi's elephant and found him missing, they assumed that he'd fallen in battle and been captured. In panic, the Shundi army scattered and retreated. Meanwhile, Goopy and Bagha regrouped with King Halla and his entourage. King Shundi was sent back to Shundi but as a punishment, his army was confiscated. Pleased with Goopy and Bagha's courage and victory, King Halla decided to marry one princess to Goopy and the other to Bagha. As his wedding gift, he gave them both his kingdom and told them to rule justly and wisely.

Days passed, and Goopy and Bagha turned out to be good, responsible rulers. One evening, as the two sat together and reflected on how their lives had changed, Bagha said, 'None of this would have happened if we hadn't met the Ghost King. He understood our music.'
Goopy nodded, 'Maybe we should visit him, have another evening of music one of these days.'
Bagha jumped up, 'What a great idea! Let's do it now!'
Before Goopy could think of a reason not to, Bagha ran in and brought out their special shoes. Then raising his hand, he prepared to chant, but hesitated.

'Er ... um ...' It had been a while since they had used it and he couldn't quite remember.
'Ah yes.
Splint splunt splont
Give us what we want ...' Bagha trailed off and looked at Goopy who raised his hand and confidently finished off the chant.
'To the Ghost King we go
With Bagha's drum in tow!'

Clap!

They found themselves in a ruin in front of a headless ghost. This was not the forest or the Ghost King they knew. The ghost sat on a rock, his severed head beside him.

'Arre!' exclaimed the headless ghost's head. 'Who are you two? Where did you come from?' Around him hovered other headless ghosts, their heads tucked under their arms or in their hands. They murmured menacingly and Goopy and Bagha quaked in their special shoes.

'Sir ... King ... I am Bagha and he is Goopy.'
'We are musicians,' said Goopy. 'We can sing for you.'
'Music, hah!' The severed head spoke in a contemptuous tone. 'And why are your heads still on your necks?'
'Your Excellency, we are not dead,' said Bagha, quickly.
'Oh, we can fix that,' said the headless Ghost-King. Nodding to a couple of headless ghosts, he told them, 'Take their heads off! And you'd better do it outside. If they are alive, blood will flow.'
'Oh no, I think we made a mistake in the spell, Goopy,' whispered Bagha.
'Yes, the one we want is the Drowned Ghost King,' replied Goopy, 'Be ready with the spell and let's get out of here.'

'Splash sploosh splish,
Give us what we wish.
Take us to the Drowned Ghost King
So the music can begin.'

Clap!

Goopy and Bagha stood in front of their old friend, the Drowned Ghost King. He recognised them and burst out laughing.

'You're still alive!'

The two friends were a bit flustered with all this talk of death.

'Remember,' continued the Ghost King, 'whenever you die, die by drowning and come straight to us. Then you can live with us forever.'

'Sir ... King ... there is some time in that ...' trailed Bagha.

'Your Highness, we don't want to die yet,' said Goopy. 'In fact, our lives have become so much better, thanks to you. We wanted to come and thank you.' 'But we made a mistake in the spell and landed up at the Headless Ghost King's,' shuddered Bagha.

'The headless ghosts!' exclaimed the Drowned Ghost King. 'Oh dear, that troupe is full of thieves, dacoits and rulers. Kings cut off the heads of dacoits, ministers cut off the heads of kings and soldiers cut off the heads of ministers. I too was a ruler – but managed to save my head.'

'Oh really? What were you the king of?'

'Of Kundi.' The Ghost King sighed, 'Alas, I was a victim of my greedy Prime Minister. He overthrew me and had me drowned in a well. He arrested my son, too. The poor boy has grown into a man, but even now he is languishing in a dungeon.' The Ghost King looked so miserable that Goopy and Bagha offered to play some music to cheer him up. When night gave way to morning and the court of the Drowned Ghost King vanished, Goopy and Bagha talked about what they had learnt. They decided to pay a visit to Kundi the next night. It was payback time!

'Splash sploosh splish,
Give us what we wish.
To Kundi we must go
And evil overthrow!'

The wicked Prime Minister lay fast asleep on the royal bed, snoring loudly. Goopy gagged him and Bagha bound his arms and legs. The Prime Minister struggled, his eyes wide with terror. But there was little he could do.

'Now what?' asked Bagha, once the Prime Minister was trussed up between them.

'Let's throw him in the same well that he threw the Ghost King in,' replied Goopy.

Clap!

Goopy and Bagha stood at the edge of the well and peered in. The water looked black and distant. Just as they were about to throw in the trussed-up Prime Minister, a voice echoed from the depths of the well.
'What are you doing? If he dies by drowning, he will come and make trouble in my troupe of ghosts.' It was the Drowned Ghost King.
'Your Highness, we are going to rescue your son,' yelled Bagha excitedly.
'I am grateful to you,' boomed the Ghost King's voice, 'But you must let justice be done. Let the new king decide what is to be done with this villain.'

So, Goopy and Bagha went to the dungeon where the Ghost King's son was being held. Dropping off the Prime Minister, they explained the situation to the young prince, and then holding his hands, they chanted their spell and arrived in the court of Kundi. The courtiers were surprised but also relieved to be rid of the evil Prime Minister. The rescued prince was crowned King, and he sentenced the Prime Minister to life imprisonment in the very same dungeon. Thanking Goopy and Bagha profusely, he asked them to stay on but it was time for them to return to Halla.

When they entered the Halla palace, they saw that it had been decorated. Shehnai was being played and servants bustled about. Just then, the old King Halla appeared.
'So there you are! We are all waiting for the fathers to begin the celebrations.'
Goopy and Bagha looked at each other uncertainly. King Halla moved aside, and behind him were the two princesses, each with a little baby in her arms.
'Aha!' thought Goopy and Bagha and burst into music. Goopy sang a celebratory raag darbari and Bagha drummed in joy. Flower petals were showered, sweets distributed and the babies held up for all to see.

And so it was that the kingdom of Halla lived happily ever after, with the music and magic of Goopy Gyne and Bagha Byne.

Copyright © 2012 Gulzar
Illustrations © 2012 Scholastic India Pvt. Ltd.
Translation © Scholastic India Pvt. Ltd.

The text for this book is abridged and translated from the original Hindi version, *Potli Baba Ki Kahani: Goopy Gyne Bagha Byne*, based on Upendrakishore Roychoudhury's *Goopy Gyne Bagha Byne*.

All rights reserved.

Published by Scholastic India Pvt. Ltd.
A subsidiary of Scholastic Inc., New York, 10012 (USA).
Publishers since 1920, with international operations in Canada,
Australia, New Zealand, the United Kingdom, India, and Hong Kong.

No part of this publication may be reproduced in whole or in part, or stored in a retrieval system, or transmitted in any form or by any means, electronic, mechanical, photocopying, recording, or otherwise without the written permission of the publisher.

For information regarding permission, write to:
Scholastic India Pvt. Ltd.
A-27, Ground Floor, Sigma Centre
Infocity-1, Sector 34, Gurgaon 122001 (ndia)

ISBN-13: 978-81-8477-844-1

First edition: May 2012

This reprint edition: December 2024

Printed in India at MicroPrints India, New Delhi